SPORTS GOATs:
THE GREATEST OF ALL TIME

GOATs OF
AUTO RACING

BY HEATHER RULE

SportsZone

An Imprint of Abdo Publishing
abdobooks.com

abdobooks.com

Published by Abdo Publishing, a division of ABDO, PO Box 398166, Minneapolis, Minnesota 55439. Copyright © 2022 by Abdo Consulting Group, Inc. International copyrights reserved in all countries. No part of this book may be reproduced in any form without written permission from the publisher. SportsZone™ is a trademark and logo of Abdo Publishing.

Printed in the United States of America, North Mankato, Minnesota.
102021
012022

THIS BOOK CONTAINS
RECYCLED MATERIALS

Cover Photo: Russell LaBounty/NKP/AP Images
Interior Photos: National Motor Museum/Heritage Images/Hulton Archive/Getty Images, 4, 4–5; Bob D'Olivo/The Enthusiast Network/Getty Images, 6, 6–7; ISC Archives/Racing One/CQ-Roll Call Group/Getty Images, 8, 8–9, 10–11, 11, 14–15, 15; ISC Images & Archives/Racing One/Getty Images, 12 (top), 13; John Lamm/The Enthusiast Network/Getty Images, 12 (bottom); Hulton Deutsch/Corbis Historical/Getty Images, 16, 16–17; AP Images, 18, 18–19; Al Messerschmidt/AP Images, 20–21, 21; Mary Ann Carter/AP Images, 22–23, 23; Doug Jennings/AP Images, 24–25, 25; Brian Cleary/Getty Images Sport/Getty Images, 26, 26–27; Mike Hewitt/Hulton Archive/Getty Images, 28, 28–29; Ben Curtis/AP Images, 30–31, 31; Jamie Squire/Getty Images Sport/Getty Images, 32 (top), 33; Focus on Sport/Getty Images, 32 (bottom); Chris Graythen/Getty Images Sport/Getty Images, 34, 34–35; Michael Conroy/AP Images, 36, 36–37; Robert Laberge/Getty Images Sport/Getty Images, 38, 38–39; Rich Graessle/Icon Sportswire/AP Images, 40–41, 41 (top); Wade Payne/AP Images, 41 (bottom); Cristiano Barni/Shutterstock Images, 42, 43

Editor: Charlie Beattie
Series Designer: Jake Nordby

Library of Congress Control Number: 2021941629

Publisher's Cataloging-in-Publication Data

Names: Rule, Heather, author.
Title: GOATs of auto racing / by Heather Rule.
Description: Minneapolis, Minnesota : Abdo Publishing, 2022 | Series: Sports GOATs: The greatest of all time | Includes online resources and index.
Identifiers: ISBN 9781532196478 (lib. bdg.) | ISBN 9781644947074 (pbk.) | ISBN 9781098218287 (ebook)
Subjects: LCSH: Automobile racing--Juvenile literature. | Speed record holders--Juvenile literature. | Automobile racing--Records--Juvenile literature. | Professional athletes--Juvenile literature.
Classification: DDC 796.72--dc23

TABLE OF CONTENTS

JUAN MANUEL FANGIO

Argentine Juan Manuel Fangio entered in the 1957 German Grand Prix seeking a fifth Formula One world championship. He was 46 years old, much older than his rivals, Peter Collins and Mike Hawthorn. A slow pit stop midway through the race put Fangio's Maserati 56 seconds behind them both.

With seven laps left, Fangio began a furious charge back into the race. During the 22-lap race he broke the track lap record 10 times. With 1 1/2 laps to go, Fangio passed Collins. He then maneuvered his way past Hawthorn for the victory. The win clinched the world championship.

Many see that race as one of the greatest drives in Formula One history. Fangio, known as the Maestro, dominated the early days of Formula One. His control of his cars was unmatched on the circuit. Fangio came into corners faster than his competitors, but the car stayed glued to the track.

Fangio's first year on the Formula One circuit was 1950. He was successful right away. That year he finished runner-up in the season standings. The next year he won his first title. A scary crash early in 1952 broke his neck, ending his season. But he returned in 1953 for another runner-up finish. For the next four years, he showed off his supreme skill. Fangio won the title every year from 1954 to 1957.

Fangio won 24 Grand Prix races in 51 starts, a record at the time. In 48 of those races, he started from the front row, including 29 times from pole position. He had the fastest race lap in 23 separate races, a record that stood for 10 years. After his 1957 title, Fangio retired as world champion.

It took 46 years for anyone to surpass Juan Manuel Fangio's record of five Formula One world championships.

A. J. FOYT

Born in Houston, A. J. Foyt earned the nickname Super Tex. But it was at Indianapolis Motor Speedway that he became a racing legend.

Foyt entered 13 United States Auto Club (USAC) (today known as IndyCar) open wheel races in 1964. He spun out in one race. In two others, he had mechanical failures. He won the rest. At Indianapolis he led the final 146 of 200 laps while averaging a then-record 147.45 miles per hour (237.30 km/h). At the end of the year, Foyt captured his fourth season championship.

Foyt's amazing 1964 was not limited to open wheel cars. He also won the Firecracker 400 stock-car race on July 4.

Foyt added Indianapolis 500 (Indy 500) wins in 1967 and again in 1977. In both races, he came from behind. In 1977 he overcame a 32-second deficit to pass Gordon Johncock late in the race. In doing so, he became the event's first four-time winner.

After a career that included a record 35 straight Indy 500 starts from 1958 to 1992, Foyt retired. On qualification day for the 1993 race, Foyt brought his car out for a ceremonial final lap. Emotional fans cheered him on as he went around the famous track one last time. His records of 67 IndyCar wins and seven season championships still stand.

FAST FACT

Foyt is the only driver to win the Indy 500, Daytona 500, and 24 Hours of Le Mans. He also won the 12 Hours of Sebring and the 24 Hours of Daytona racing sports cars.

A. J. Foyt poses in front of the famous Borg-Warner Trophy after winning the 1964 Indianapolis 500.

RICHARD PETTY

NASCAR is a sport rooted in outlaw culture. No racer has looked the part more than Richard Petty. His signature look of a black cowboy hat, gator-skin boots, and dark sunglasses is recognized by racing fans everywhere.

He is also racing royalty. Petty's father, Lee, won the first Daytona 500 in 1959. Richard soon started winning himself. Along the way, he earned the nickname the Randleman Rocket, a reference to his hometown of Randleman, North Carolina.

By 1967 Petty was making history. He won 27 NASCAR Cup races in 48 starts that year. That included 10 straight from August 12 to October 1. None of his wins were even close. Driving his bright blue 1966 Plymouth Belvedere, he won four races by at least three laps. Early in the year, he won his fifty-fifth race. That broke a tie with his father for the most in NASCAR history. By the end of the year, he had earned a new nickname: the King.

That nickname stuck over the course of a legendary 35-year career. Petty entered 1,184 races and won 200. The driver in second place, David Pearson, is 95 wins behind. Petty's total included a record seven wins at the Daytona 500.

FAST FACT

Petty finished in the top 10 in NASCAR points standings for 19 straight years (1966 to 1985). His streak could have been longer. He only ran 14 races in 1965 when he spent time drag racing.

Richard Petty's blue-and-red No. 43 car is one of the most recognizable in racing history.

CALE YARBOROUGH

Many successful drivers had dynasties. Cale Yarborough's came in the late 1970s. The energetic, aggressive driver won 28 races during the 1976 through 1978 NASCAR seasons and took home all three championships. No driver had won three straight before Yarborough. His streak stood as a record until Jimmie Johnson won five in a row from 2006 to 2010.

In an odd way, the South Carolina-born Yarborough helped put NASCAR on the national map. The 1979 Daytona 500 was the first time a race was live on national television. That meant it was the first time that fans outside the sport's mostly southern home could see the action of a race. On the final lap, Yarborough and Donnie Allison were all alone up on the backstretch for the lead. Their cars touched four times before they crashed into the wall.

The racers ended up in the infield. Allison and Yarborough got out and exchanged words. When Donnie's brother Bobby came over, Yarborough started yelling and then hit Bobby in the face with a race helmet. The fight was called NASCAR's "first big deal" by race winner Richard Petty. That race, and the fight, are often credited with creating NASCAR's boom in popularity over the following decade.

Among his 83 career wins, Yarborough claimed four Daytona 500 victories. They came in three different decades. His last two came back-to-back in 1983 and 1984.

Cale Yarborough holds up the trophy after winning his final Daytona 500, in 1984.

DAVID PEARSON

Richard Petty snuck ahead of David Pearson's car out of turn four on the final lap of the 1976 Daytona 500. Their cars were so close that they made contact. Both racers hit the wall. Then they both spun short of the finish line. Pearson made a last-ditch effort for the checkered flag. Cutting across the infield grass, he made it across the line for the win.

It was one of the most memorable finishes to the Daytona 500. It was also Pearson's only win in the sport's most famous event. But it was not the only time the Spartanburg, South Carolina, native got the best of his main rival, Petty. The two finished first and second in 63 races. Pearson won 33 of those.

When Pearson's career ended in 1989, the racer they called the Silver Fox ranked second on NASCAR's list with 105 career victories. That total came in only 574 starts. Even though he raced for nearly as long as Petty, Pearson entered roughly half the number of races. Petty won a total of 200 races. But he believed their totals would be closer if Pearson had raced more often. Pearson entered, and won, enough races to claim season championships in 1966, 1968, and 1969.

Pearson (21) and Richard Petty race side by side at the 1974 Daytona 500. The two legends enjoyed a long and respectful rivalry.

David Pearson entered only 19 of 30 races during the 1974 NASCAR season, yet he still finished third in the points standings.

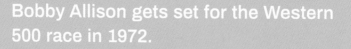

Bobby Allison gets set for the Western 500 race in 1972.

BOBBY ALLISON

In the late 1950s, Bobby Allison, his brother Donnie, and friend Red Farmer were living in Alabama. The trio had great success racing at dirt tracks throughout the state. One day, as they entered a racetrack in North Carolina, a rival racer called out, "Here comes that dang Alabama Gang." The name stuck throughout Bobby Allison's long, storied career.

The Miami-born Allison reached the NASCAR circuit in the early 1960s, but it took him a long time to become a winner. He was runner-up five times in the 1970s and early 1980s. That included a 1972 season in which Allison won 10 races and finished second another 12 times.

It all came together in 1983. He won one race in a Chevrolet. Then he switched to a Buick and won five more. Heading into the season's final day, he needed to stay ahead of Darrell Waltrip for the season title. Tire problems kept Allison from contending, but he raced well enough to finish ninth and hold off Waltrip.

Allison's storied career saw him win all four major NASCAR races: the Winston 500, Daytona 500, Coca-Cola 600, and Southern 500. He won each race at least three times.

In February 1988, he captured his third Daytona 500, with his son Davey finishing second. A violent crash at Pocono Raceway in June 1988 sadly left Bobby Allison with career-ending injuries and memory loss. He retired as third on the all-time wins list.

JACKIE STEWART

Jackie Stewart's car hit standing water at 170 miles per hour (274 km/h) during the 1966 Formula One Belgian Grand Prix. The car went off an eight-foot (2.4-m) drop and landed upside down. There were no safety crews at the track to help. Instead, drivers Graham Hill and Bob Bondurant, who also crashed, rescued Stewart.

That crash helped Stewart see what safety improvements were needed in racing. In those days, very few tracks even had safety barriers along the side of the track. Stewart spent the rest of his career battling race authorities to improve conditions. He even organized a boycott of the German Grand Prix in 1970 when he thought the track was unsafe. Officials gave in and moved the race.

Stewart's career lasted only nine years, from 1965 to 1973. But the Scotsman accomplished quite a bit in a short time. At the time, rookies rarely won races, but Stewart took first at the Italian Grand Prix in his first season. Within four years, he was world champion. Stewart would capture two more world championship titles, in 1971 and 1973.

After a teammate died in a crash during a qualifying run on October 6, 1973, Stewart retired. He took up his safety campaign full time. For five years, Stewart served as the president of the Grand Prix Drivers' Association. Many of today's Formula One safety measures exist because of Stewart's tireless efforts.

Jackie Stewart started only 99 races in his Formula One career but won 27 of them.

MARIO ANDRETTI

Born in Italy, Mario Andretti moved to rural Pennsylvania as a teenager. He and his twin brother, Aldo, loved racing. But their father did not. They had to keep their driving dreams a secret. However, when Aldo ended up in the hospital after a crash, the secret was out. Mario kept racing, and sixty years later the Andretti name is one of the most recognizable in motorsports.

Mario Andretti was one of racing's most versatile drivers. He is one of only two drivers to have won races in Formula One, IndyCar, World Sportscar Championship, and NASCAR. He won four IndyCar titles and finished his career second only to A. J. Foyt in career IndyCar wins.

Despite his success in IndyCar, Andretti won the Indy 500 only once. After his lone win in 1969, his long quest to win again became known as the Andretti Curse. He entered the race 24 more times but finished only seven. In two of those, he finished second.

Andretti still had plenty of success. He won the 12 Hours of Sebring racing sports cars in 1967, 1970, and 1972. In 1978 he showed even more versatility by winning the Formula One season championship.

Milestone wins continued into the 1990s for Andretti. At age 53, he won the 1993 IndyCar race at Phoenix. The victory made him the oldest IndyCar winner ever.

Mario retired from full-time racing in 1994, but the Andretti name did not leave the sport. His sons Jeff and Michael, nephew John, and grandson Marco have all enjoyed successful careers.

Mario Andretti waves to the crowd after his only Indianapolis 500 win, in 1969.

Al Unser Sr. earned 28 pole positions and recorded 39 wins during his long open wheel racing career.

AL UNSER SR.

Other IndyCar drivers in 1970 barely stood a chance with Al Unser Sr. on the track. He won 10 of 18 races, including his first Indy 500, and finished in the top five 16 times. He led 69 percent of all laps run that season.

Unser was born in Albuquerque, New Mexico. Hailing from one of the most successful families in racing, he began his own racing career in 1957. Eight years later, in 1965, he made his Indy 500 debut. At Indy Unser made himself a legend. His 1970 win was followed by another in 1971. And yet another win followed in 1978.

By 1987 he was 47 years old, and he entered race week without a team. Ultimately replacing an injured driver, Unser started in twentieth position. He slowly made his way through the field and led the last 18 laps. After crossing the finish line for the win, Unser became the second driver to win the Indy 500 four times. He also broke his brother Bobby's record as the oldest driver to win the race.

In addition to the win, his final lap set a record for most laps led in the history of the race, with 613. His record would extend to 644 by the time he retired in 1994.

FAST FACT

Al Unser Sr. and Bobby Unser are the only brothers who have both won the Indy 500. Al's son, Al Unser Jr., has also won it twice. In addition Al Unser Sr.'s brother Jerry and nephews Robby and Johnny have all competed in the famous race.

Rick Mears salutes the crowd after winning his third Indianapolis 500, in 1988.

RICK MEARS

I n 1978 IndyCar team owner Roger Penske needed a driver to fill in while Mario Andretti was racing in Formula One. He called on 1976 IndyCar Rookie of the Year Rick Mears. After Mears won three races that season, Penske decided to make him a full-time driver. The man they called Rocket Rick was an Indy 500 champion a year later.

Over the next 12 years, the Kansas native showed his early success was no fluke. By 1991 he joined A. J. Foyt and Al Unser Sr. as the only four-time winners at Indianapolis. Mears could have had two more wins if not for some close finishes.

In 1982 Mears led 77 laps before falling behind Gordon Johncock. With 13 laps to go, Johncock led by 12 seconds. But Mears made a furious charge, erasing almost a second from the lead on every lap. On the first turn of the final lap, Mears nearly passed Johncock. Only a last-ditch maneuver by Johncock kept Mears in second place. In the end, Johncock won by 0.16 seconds. It was the closest-ever Indy 500 finish at the time. Mears also contended in 1986 but fell just short.

The 1991 race came down to the wire again, but this time Mears outlasted Michael Andretti at the end. The two exchanged passes late in the race after a restart before Mears held on. The win made Mears the only driver to have won the race from pole position in three different decades. Through 2021 his record of six pole position starts at Indianapolis still stood.

DARRELL WALTRIP

Darrell Waltrip had 16 NASCAR wins under his belt before what he called the best drive of his career. The race was the 1979 Rebel 500 at Darlington, South Carolina. Waltrip and Richard Petty swapped the lead 10 times in the race. They went back and forth four times on the final lap alone.

When the checkered flag flew, Waltrip crossed the line before Petty. The win was a confidence boost for Waltrip, who had dethroned the King.

When the Kentucky-born Waltrip came onto the driving scene, he clashed with several drivers. Petty said the fastest thing about Waltrip was his mouth. Waltrip was given the nickname Jaws by Cale Yarborough for his outspoken manner.

Waltrip backed up his talk with excellent racing. His 84 NASCAR Cup victories are tied for fourth on the all-time list with Bobby Allison. Waltrip won season titles in 1981, 1982, and 1985. In 1989 he took home his only Daytona 500 win. Waltrip's 59 pole position starts are fifth-most in history.

After retiring in 2000, Waltrip started a 20-year career as a broadcaster. In the television booth, his enthusiastic personality made him an instant hit with fans. The first race he announced was the 2001 Daytona 500, won by his brother Michael.

Darrell Waltrip hollers to the crowd after winning the 1989 Daytona 500.

DALE EARNHARDT SR.

The Daytona 500 is the race every NASCAR driver wants to win. By 1998 Dale Earnhardt had won everything else. He was a seven-time season champion. Three times he won back-to-back season titles. But the Intimidator, as he was known, had lost many close races at Daytona. He had led the 500 with 10 laps left four times, but he had never come away with a win.

The 46-year-old Earnhardt came into the 1998 race on a 59-race winless streak. Late in the race, he again held the lead when a crash brought on a caution. Under the yellow and checkered flags, Earnhardt finally won the Daytona 500. Fans in the packed stands raised three fingers for Earnhardt's No. 3 black car. Crew workers from every race team lined up to greet him as he drove slowly down pit road. It was the crowning achievement of an amazing career.

Earnhardt would sadly lose his life on the same Daytona track in 2001. It was the 676th race of a career that started in 1975, but on the final lap his car grazed a fellow racer and careened into the wall at 180 miles per hour (290 km/h). He suffered head injuries and died at a Florida hospital hours later.

FAST FACT

Earnhardt's death led to new racing safety measures. By October 2001, all NASCAR drivers had to wear a Head and Neck Support (HANS) device that attaches to a driver's helmet. Championship Auto Racing Teams (CART), what is now IndyCar, mandated the HANS device on all tracks in 1999.

Dale Earnhardt won his first NASCAR season title in 1980 and his last in 1994.

AYRTON SENNA

At the starting line of the 1988 Formula One Japanese Grand Prix, Ayrton Senna's clutch failed. Other drivers flew past him. When he finally got his car going, Senna was 10 seconds behind his teammate and rival, Alain Prost. The two were locked in a battle for the Formula One championship. Senna quickly got to work. He passed driver after driver as he worked his way back.

On lap 28 out of 51, Senna finally made his move and passed Prost for the lead. One of his greatest drives also meant his first Formula One world championship.

Senna was the fastest Formula One driver the world had seen. The handsome Brazilian was a natural racing talent. He won eight times with 13 pole positions in 16 races in his 1988 championship season. He earned two more titles in 1990 and 1991. Senna won 41 of the 161 Grand Prix races he entered.

Like several other great drivers, Senna's life was taken in a crash. He was leading a race May 1, 1994, at a track in Imola, Italy, when his Williams-Renault struck a wall at 145 miles per hour (233 km/h). After his death, the Brazilian government declared three days of national mourning for the country's racing hero.

FAST FACT

Senna loved children. He gave millions of dollars from his personal fortune to underprivileged kids in Brazil. After his death, his sister Viviane created the Ayrton Senna Institute to help Brazilian children reach their potential through quality education.

Ayrton Senna won the famous Monaco Grand Prix six times, including five in a row from 1989 to 1993.

Michael Schumacher returned to the Formula One circuit in 2010 after briefly retiring three years earlier.

MICHAEL SCHUMACHER

Torrential rain pounded the track the day of the 1996 Spanish Grand Prix. Conditions were tough for every driver, including the two-time defending Formula One champion, Michael Schumacher.

The track was so slick that pole sitter Damon Hill spun twice in the first nine laps. Schumacher started in third position but dropped several spots before claiming the lead on lap 13. He never looked back. Schumacher turned laps five seconds faster than any other driver. The victory was one of the greatest wet-weather drives ever.

Schumacher was a racing prodigy. The German won his first championship at age six in go-kart racing. During his dominant Formula One stretch in the early 2000s, he was noted for his intelligence and feel for driving. Schumacher was known for rarely making mistakes.

Juan Manuel Fangio's record of five Formula One titles had stood since 1957. But in 2003, Schumacher looked to break it. Driving for Ferrari, he defended his title against several challengers, winning six races. On the last day of the season, Schumacher's eighth-place finish was good enough to hold off Finland's Kimi Raikkonen by two points for the record-breaking title.

Schumacher cemented his legacy the next year by winning 13 of 18 races. His seventh title came by 34 points over teammate Rubens Barrichello.

FAST FACT

Schumacher's younger brother, Ralf, was also a successful driver who won six times in his 11-year career. The Schumachers are the only set of brothers to both win Formula One races.

JEFF GORDON

Jeff Gordon grew up far away from NASCAR's southern roots. He lived in California until he was 15, then he moved to Indiana looking for more racing opportunities. At one point, he wanted to be an IndyCar driver, but he could never find a team. He linked up with NASCAR in 1990 and joined the Cup series two years later.

Gordon took the circuit by storm. He was just 24 when he won his first season championship in 1995. That made him the youngest driver to win since Bill Rexford in 1950. When Gordon won his third season title in 1998, he won 13 of 33 races and had 28 top-10 finishes. He added a fourth and final title in 2001.

Gordon retired in 2016 after entering 805 races, including a NASCAR record streak of 797 in a row. His 93 wins are third-most of all time, and he won the Daytona 500 three times. Over the course of his career, Gordon led nearly 25,000 laps.

Gordon's success changed NASCAR. Big-money sponsors lined up to support the growing sport. Fans came from all over the country. The drivers did too. Before Gordon very few drivers grew up outside the southern United States. By the time he retired in 2016, the roster of 40 drivers on the circuit included seven Californians as well as drivers from Connecticut, Idaho, Washington, and Michigan.

Gordon (24) duels Dale Earnhardt Sr. at the 1993 Daytona 500. The two drivers enjoyed one of the sport's best rivalries during the 1990s.

Jeff Gordon was voted into the Motorsports Hall of Fame of America in 2018 and the NASCAR Hall of Fame the following year.

JIMMIE JOHNSON

From 1976 to 1978, Cale Yarborough won three consecutive NASCAR Cup championships. Over the next three decades, three drivers managed to win back-to-back titles, but no one could match Yarborough's feat. That changed when Jimmie Johnson came along.

From 2006 to 2010, the California native racked up a record five straight championships. Racing against a deep and talented field of drivers, Johnson won 35 races during his dominant stretch.

The 2007 season was Johnson's best. He won 10 races and captured the NASCAR Cup title by 77 points. Two years later, his margin of victory was 141 points. After the 2009 season, the Associated Press named Johnson its Male Athlete of the Year. He was the first driver ever to win the award.

Entering the final race of the 2010 Cup playoff, Johnson's streak was in trouble. He trailed leader Denny Hamlin by 15 points in the standings. Hamlin struggled with damage to his car for most of the race. Johnson took advantage, coming on late to finish the race second. Hamlin dropped to fourteenth place, and Johnson took his fifth season title by 39 points. Many drivers and journalists considered Johnson's championship streak a record that would never be broken.

Johnson went on to add two more season titles, in 2013 and 2016, before leaving NASCAR for good after the 2020 season. His seven championships tied Richard Petty and Dale Earnhardt Sr. for the most of all time.

From his rookie year in 2002 until 2014, Jimmie Johnson never finished lower than sixth in the NASCAR season standings.

HELIO CASTRONEVES

Helio Castroneves broke into open wheel racing with the CART circuit in the late 1990s. He won his first race at Belle Isle in Detroit in 2000. After crossing the finish line, the 25-year-old jumped out of his car. He ran over to the fence separating the track from the supporters and scaled it. Fans soon got used to the sight of Castroneves climbing the fence after his wins. They nicknamed him Spider-Man.

Castroneves's signature celebration matched the Brazilian driver's flashy personality. Known for his seemingly permanent smile, Castroneves became one of the sport's most popular racers.

Castroneves switched over to the IndyCar circuit in 2001. There he could race in the Indy 500. Not many drivers get their first IndyCar win in the series' biggest race. But Castroneves did, leading the final 52 laps to win his first Indy 500 in 2001. He showed it was no fluke by doing it again in 2002.

After winning his third Indy 500 in 2009, Castroneves was just one shy of the record held by A. J. Foyt, Al Unser Sr., and Rick Mears. But it looked like he might never reach the mark, especially when he became a part-time driver in 2018. He entered the 2021 Indy 500 starting from the eighth spot. The 46-year-old slowly worked his way up to the front and dramatically passed young driver Alex Palou on the final lap for the win.

After the race, Castroneves stopped his car in front of the famous yard of bricks at the start/finish line and climbed a race fence for the thirty-first time. His entire crew joined the celebration.

Helio Castroneves holds up the traditional milk bottle enjoyed by the Indianapolis 500 winner after his first victory at the famous race, in 2001.

SCOTT DIXON

Most drivers struggle to maintain success after the age of 40. In 2020 Scott Dixon proved he was not most drivers. Dixon claimed his sixth IndyCar title, edging Josef Newgarten by 16 points. He was the first driver in his 40s to win the season title since 1993. The victory left him one shy of A. J. Foyt's record of seven IndyCar championships.

It was nothing new for Dixon, who began racing go-karts at age seven in his native New Zealand. He was so good that he was allowed to enter road races at age 13. New Zealanders have to be 15 to get a driver's license, so Dixon needed a special exemption to start so young.

He came to the United States in 2001 and brought his winning ways with him. His first victory came at Nazareth Speedway in Pennsylvania on May 6, 2001. At 20 years old, Dixon became the youngest driver ever to win an IndyCar race.

Dixon was never the flashiest driver. But over the years, he developed a reputation for consistency. In 2006 he was the only driver to finish every race of the IndyCar season. Three years later, he ran 2,766 out of a possible 2,788 laps, leading all drivers. As of 2021, he had won at least one race in 17 straight seasons.

Dixon made Indianapolis his adopted home, and he captured his first Indy 500 in 2008. That year he also took home his second season championship. After he won his fifth season title in 2018, the mayor of Indianapolis declared September 24 "Scott Dixon Day" in the city.

Scott Dixon was awarded the New Zealand Order of Merit in 2019 for his contributions to racing.

Kyle Busch's fiery competitive streak often led to run-ins with other drivers, on and off the track.

KYLE BUSCH

Kyle Busch's aggressive nature, both on and off the track, have not always won him fans. His driving style earned him the nickname Wild Thing. Many times his actions led to run-ins with other drivers, sometimes even fights. But it also won him many races during a career that was still going strong into the 2020s.

Busch's two NASCAR Cup titles both came the hard way. In 2015 he suffered an injury in a February crash that forced him to miss nearly three months. At the end of the season, he held off rival Kevin Harvick by a single point.

In 2019 Busch started the year on a roll. He won four of the first 14 races. He then went 21 races without a victory. Only a dramatic win in the season's final race at Homestead-Miami Speedway gave him the season title. He beat Martin Truex Jr. by only five points in the standings.

The Las Vegas native's 59 NASCAR Cup wins led all active drivers as of September 2021. He was still a long way from Richard Petty's record of 200. But Busch also raced, and won, often on NASCAR's two second-level circuits. He added 162 wins there as well.

Total cup wins are not the only comparison between Busch and Petty. Busch's first win of 2021 gave him victories in 17 consecutive seasons, one shy of Petty's 18.

Kyle Busch celebrates his 2011 win at Bristol Raceway, one of his four NASCAR wins that season.

LEWIS HAMILTON

Over the course of his career, Michael Schumacher won 91 Formula One races. It was thought to be an unbeatable record. That was until English racing prodigy Lewis Hamilton came along.

Hamilton started racing at the age of eight. By 2007 the 22-year-old was debuting on the Formula One circuit. Right away he began smashing records, setting rookie marks for wins, poles, and points.

The next year, he won it all in dramatic fashion. At the season's final race in Brazil, Hamilton passed another driver on the final corner to move into fifth place. That earned him enough points to secure the season championship. He was the youngest driver ever to claim a Formula One title.

In the 2010s, the sight of Hamilton on the podium became a yearly event. While enjoying heated rivalries with fellow drivers Nico Rosberg and Sebastian Vettel, Hamilton won six of the seven season titles between 2014 and 2020. His total of seven matched Schumacher's record. In Portugal in 2020, Hamilton won his 92nd career race, passing the record most thought Schumacher would hold forever.

Hamilton accomplished all of this while battling prejudice at every turn. As Formula One's only Black driver, he encountered racism at

FAST FACT

In 1995 Hamilton was a 10-year-old kart champ. He wrote a note to Ron Dennis, the boss of the McLaren Mercedes Formula One team, saying he'd like to race for Dennis's team one day. Dennis called Hamilton three years later and offered money to support Hamilton's career.

several races. He also struggled to gain acceptance in his own country. Because of this, Hamilton has been a vocal activist for change. For his efforts on and off the track, he was knighted by Queen Elizabeth II at the end of 2020.

In 2021 Lewis Hamilton became the first Formula One driver in history to earn 100 career pole positions.

HONORABLE MENTIONS

BOBBY UNSER

The Colorado native won 37 open wheel races between 1966 and 1981. He's also a three-time Indy 500 winner (1968, 1975, 1981).

PHIL HILL

Hill was the first American driver to become the Formula One World Champion when he won in 1961. He also won the 24 Hours of Le Mans three times.

DAN GURNEY

The versatile Gurney won seven IndyCar races, five NASCAR races, and four Formula One races from 1962 to 1970.

NIKI LAUDA

The Austrian won three Formula One titles, including two following a serious crash in 1976 that left him badly burned and nearly cost him his life.

JANET GUTHRIE

The Iowa-born Guthrie was the first woman to qualify for and race in the Indy 500 in 1977. She was also the first woman to race NASCAR's Daytona 500, finishing twelfth in 1977 and eleventh in 1980.

JAMES HUNT

The often reckless British driver captured 10 wins in just 93 races over his short six-year career, including the 1976 Formula One season championship.

ALAIN PROST

The Frenchman won 51 of his 202 career Formula One races, and he captured four season titles between 1985 and 1993.

DANICA PATRICK

Patrick was the first woman to lead the Indy 500. She led 19 laps and finished fourth as a rookie at the 2005 Indy 500. She was also the first woman to win an open wheel race and a NASCAR Cup Series pole position.

GLOSSARY

boycott
Refusing to purchase a product or take part in an event as a form of protest.

caution
A segment of a race in which racers cannot pass each other, usually because of a crash or debris on the track.

checkered flag
A black-and-white flag with a checkered pattern that is waved at the end of a race. The driver to cross the line first under this flag is the winner.

circuit
A group of racing teams that compete against each other.

exemption
A special rule that frees someone from a requirement.

Grand Prix
Another name for a Formula One race. It comes from the French language and means "great prize."

maneuver
A skilled move.

pole position
The most favorable position at the start of an auto race, typically in the inside of the front row.

prodigy
A young athlete who has a great natural ability for a sport.

qualifying
An event in which drivers run laps on a track to see which position they will start for that race.

rival
An opponent with whom a player or team has a fierce and ongoing competition.

stock car
A race car that looks like a car seen on the road.

MORE INFORMATION

BOOKS

Hewson, Anthony K. *Innovations in Auto Racing*. Minneapolis, MN: Abdo Publishing, 2022.

Marquardt, Meg. *STEM in Auto Racing*. Minneapolis, MN: Abdo Publishing, 2018.

Rule, Heather. *Ultimate NASCAR Road Trip*. Minneapolis, MN: Abdo Publishing, 2019.

ONLINE RESOURCES

Booklinks
NONFICTION NETWORK
FREE! ONLINE NONFICTION RESOURCES

To learn more about the GOATs of auto racing, please visit **abdobooklinks.com** or scan this QR code. These links are routinely monitored and updated to provide the most current information available.

INDEX

ABOUT THE AUTHOR

Heather Rule is a freelance sports journalist, author, and social media coordinator. She has a bachelor's degree in journalism and mass communication from the University of St. Thomas.